This Book Belongs To :

____

____

Coloring Me!

Coloring Me!

Coloring Me!

Coloring Me!

Coloring Me!

Coloring Me!

Coloring Me!

Coloring Me!

Coloring Me!

Coloring Me!

Coloring Me!

Coloring Me!

Coloring Me!

Coloring Me!

Coloring Me!

Coloring Me!

Coloring Me!

Coloring Me!

Coloring Me!

COLORING ME!

Coloring Me!

Coloring Me!

Coloring Me!

Coloring Me!

Coloring Me!

Coloring Me!

Coloring Me!

Coloring Me!

Coloring Me!

Coloring Me!

Coloring Me!

Coloring Me!

Coloring Me!

Coloring Me!

Coloring Me!

Coloring Me!

Coloring Me!

Coloring Me!

Coloring Me!

Coloring Me!

Coloring Me!

Coloring Me!

Coloring Me!

Coloring Me!

Coloring Me!

Coloring Me!

Coloring Me!

Coloring Me!

Coloring Me!

Animals Coloring Book
by **CARTA Publishing**

Cover and interior images copyright **Freepik**
and **creativefabrica**, User "Fox Design Studio"

For any suggestions or questions regarding our books,
plaese contact us at : cartapublishing@gmail.com

Without your voice we don't exist.
Please, support us and leave a review!

Thank you!